BERGER & WYSE

*I like Berger and Wyse cartoons and I like food,
so I particularly like Berger and Wyse food cartoons.*
Hugh Fearnley-Whittingstall

*Berger and Wyse's dark dry cartoons about food would
be the ultimate thing of goodness, if they weren't so nakedly sproutist.*
John Lanchester

Bringing ingredients to life in ways that we chefs can't even aspire to.
Allegra McEvedy

Clever, witty, funny and pointed; rare qualities in the food world.
Matthew Fort

BERGER & WYSE

Collected food cartoons from the *Guardian*

Absolute Press

First published in Great Britain in 2011
by Absolute Press
Scarborough House
29 James Street West
Bath BA1 2BT
Phone 44 (0) 1225 316013
Fax 44 (0) 1225 445836
E-mail info@absolutepress.co.uk
Website www.absolutepress.co.uk

Publisher Jon Croft
Commissioning Editor Meg Avent
Art Direction Matt Inwood
Design Claire Siggery

A catalogue record of this book is available from the
British Library.

ISBN 9781906650612

Printed and bound on behalf of Latitude Press in China.

A note about the text
This book is set in Sabon MT. Sabon was designed by
Jan Tschichold in 1964. The roman design is based on
type by Claude Garamond, whereas the italic design is
based on types by Robert Granjon. All hand-written
elements from the hand of Joe Berger.

To Charlotte and Helen, our taste testers.

Berger and Wyse first met in a lift, having stormed out of meetings with their respective agents, who had struggled to find publishers for their pioneering condition-specific cookbooks (Wyse's *Zimmer Gently – Recipes for the Elderly* and Berger's *Strain into Bowl – Colonic Gastronomy*). The pair drowned their sorrows over a three-martini lunch, and Berger and Wyse stumbled into being.

They have since produced animation and comic strips for various outlets, including Channel 4, BBC, Sky, Discovery, and the *Guardian*. Their title sequence to BBC1's *Hustle* secured Bafta, Emmy and RTS nominations, none of which was won and often involved expensive nights at award ceremonies.

Their four-panel strip *The Pitchers*, a portrayal of the film business that occasionally managed to be more stupid than Hollywood itself, ran in the *Guardian* for six years. The food cartoons featured in this book are part of an ongoing series that appears weekly in the *Guardian Weekend* magazine.

Strain into Bowl is currently being turned in to an action feature film by Panaversal Pictures, produced by Larry Goldnutz.

Nº· 102 | November 2009

N⁰· 24 | March 2008

IN ACTUAL FACT, IT'S THE METHYLTHIOALKYLISOTHIOCYANATES IN THE ROCKET LEAVES WHICH, IN COMBINATION WITH THE SULPHUR METABOLISM COMMON TO ALL BRASSICACEAE, PRODUCES THE CHARACTERISTIC PUNGENT FLAVOUR. SO, TECHNICALLY SPEAKING...
OK OK, IT IS ROCKET SCIENCE. JUST HURRY IT UP!

Nº 67 | February 2009

Nº· 55 | October 2008

Nº· 163 | March 2011

Nº 39 | July 2008

Nᵒ 56 | November 2008

Nᵒ· 59 | November 2008

Nᵒ· 64 | January 2008

Nº 73 | March 2009

ONE APPLE, TWO PEARS, THREE PLUMS, FOUR STRAWBERRIES, FIVE ORANGES, ONE PIECE OF CHOCOLATE CAKE, ONE ICE CREAM CONE, ONE PICKLE, ONE SLICE OF SWISS CHEESE, ONE SLICE OF SALAMI, ONE LOLLIPOP, ONE PIECE OF CHERRY PIE, ONE SAUSAGE, ONE CUPCAKE, ONE SLICE OF WATERMELON AND ONE NICE GREEN LEAF, TABLE TWELVE...

N⁰· 01 | September 2007

N°. 77 | April 2009

N°· 80 | May 2009

Nᵒ· 97 | September 2009

Nº· 83 | May 2009

Nᵒ· 38 | June 2008

N⁰· 87 | June 2009

N°. 90 | August 2009

N°· 91 | August 2009

Nᵒ 94 | September 2009

Nᵒ· 41 | July 2008

Nᵒ 99 | October 2009

Nᵒ· 104 | December 2009

Nº· 109 | February 2010

Nᵒ· 16 | January 2008

Nº 111 | March 2010

Nᵒ· 114 | April 2010

Nº· 39 | July 2008

N°. 118 | April 2010

Nº 121 | May 2010

N⁰· 127 | June 2010

Nº 15 | January 2008

N°· 131 | August 2010

No. 132 | August 2010

Nº 137 | September 2010

Nᵒ· 29 | May 2008

N⁰· 138 | September 2010

Nᵒ· 145 | November 2010

Nº 146 | November 2010

Nº 26 | April 2008

N⁰· 147 | November 2010

N°· 149 | December 2010

Nᵒ· 151 | January 2011

N°. 02 | October 2007

N⁰· 152 | December 2010

Nº· 153 | January 2011

N⁰· 157 | February 2011

Nº· 11 | December 2007

I BLACKED OUT, WOKE UP UNDER THE FRIDGE... ALL I CAN THINK ABOUT NOW IS WHY ME? WHY DID I SURVIVE, WHEN THOUSANDS PERISHED?
WE CAN ALL RELATE TO THAT.
MMM...

N⁰· 167 | April 2011

Nᵒ· 159 | February 2011

Nᵒ· 170 | May 2011

N⁰· 04 | October 2007

Many thanks to Merope Mills for giving the cartoons a home in the
Guardian Weekend magazine – plus Bob and the rest of the *Weekend* team for their
production help. Thank you also to friends, readers and family who encourage us
weekly – and make it clear when they have no idea what the joke is supposed to be.
For their words of support, we're grateful to Hugh Fearnley-Whittingstall,
John Lanchester, Allegra McEvedy and Matthew Fort. Finally, thanks to Jon Croft
and Matt Inwood at Absolute Press for their flattering enthusiasm, and for publishing
the book you are holding.